VACATION
Activity Book

ALAIN GRÉE

Button
BOOKS

Vacation essentials

What might you take on vacation? Choose from the list and write the answers underneath each item. The words left behind are some other things you might need, depending on whether it's summer or winter. Write them on the lines below.

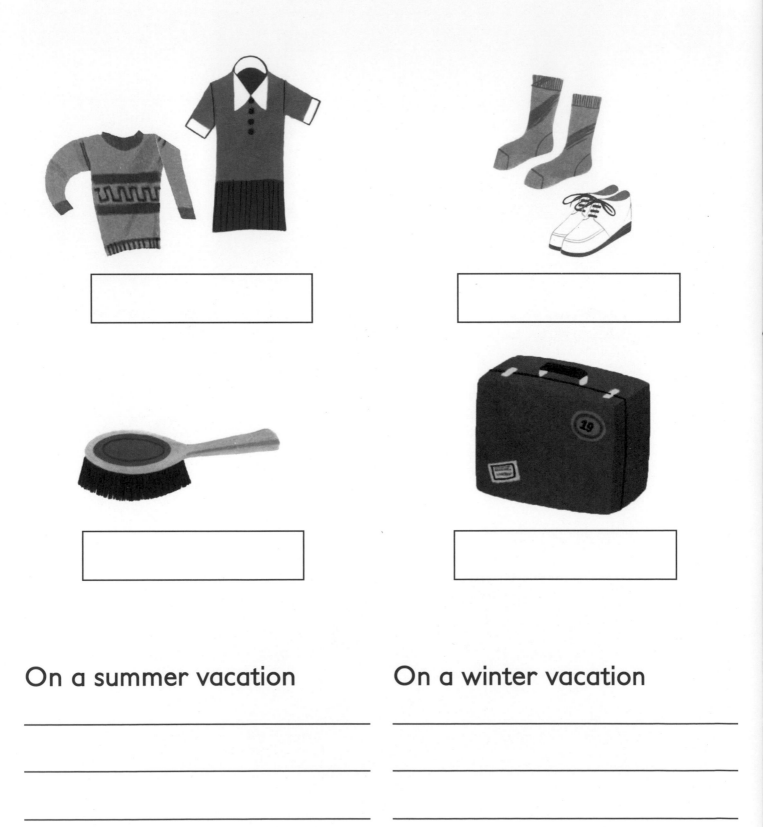

On a summer vacation

_____

_____

_____

On a winter vacation

_____

_____

_____

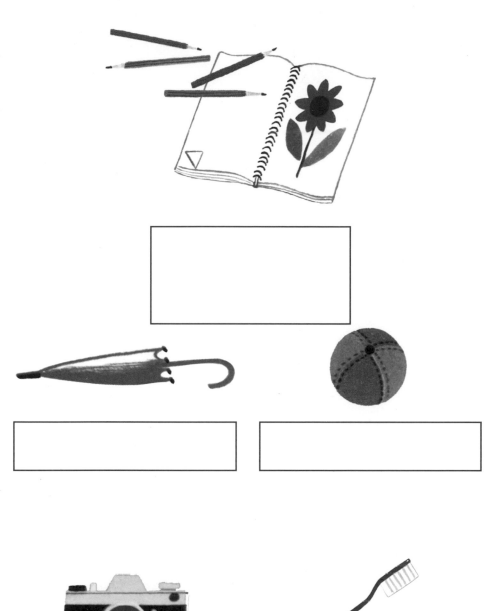

shoes and socks

suitcase

scarf

toothpaste

sun hat

toothbrush

umbrella

clothes

sunscreen

ball

gloves

hairbrush

warm hat

camera

bathing suit

coloring pencils
and notebook

Beach fun

How many people can you see in the picture? How many boats are there?
How many balls? Add some stickers from the center of the book if you like.

◯ people   ◯ boats   ◯ balls

Getting around

How do you travel around when you go on vacation? There are lots of ways you can get about. Can you fill in the missing letters to name them?

ta_i

b_c_cle

w_lk_ng

b__t

c_r

sc__ter

Traveling by bus

The bus driver is picking people up to take them on a day trip.
Find the stickers in the center of this book to add the passengers.

Going on vacation by train

Look at the picture. How many people can you see on the train? How many people are on the platform? How many dogs can you see? Write your answers in the circles below.

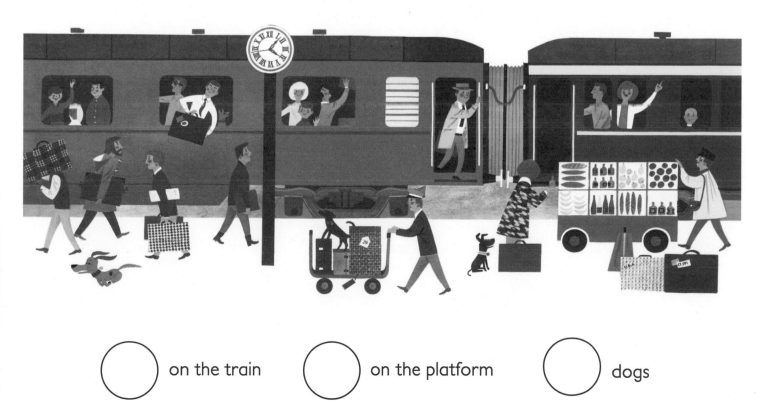

◯ on the train ◯ on the platform ◯ dogs

Name the place

Can you label these European countries? Choose from the list and write the numbers in the boxes. If you know any more countries, write their names on the map.

1 France
2 Italy
3 Greece
4 Spain
5 Portugal
6 Germany
7 Denmark
8 Ireland
9 England
10 Scotland

Find the lighthouse

If you go to the seashore you may see a lighthouse. This shines a bright light to help ships avoid crashing into rocks! Join the dots to complete this picture and then color it in. Use different colors to form stripes.

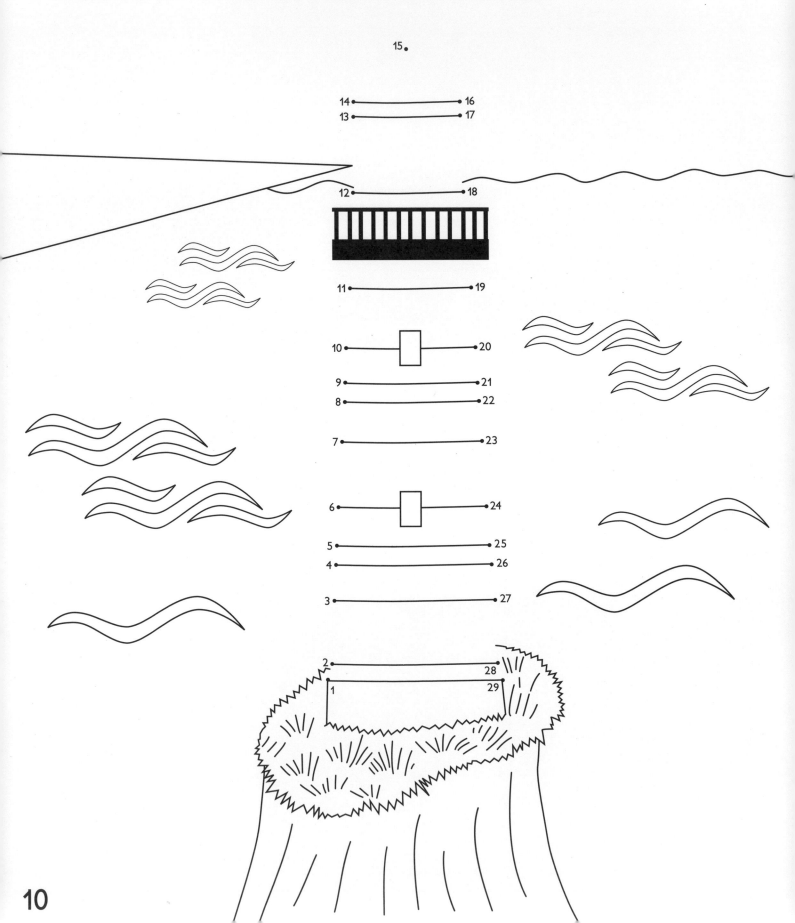

Beach game

In this beach game the volleyball goes from player 1 to player 6 in sequence.
Draw lines between the players to show where the ball goes.

Which color team has odd numbers?

Which color team has even numbers?

Costume mix-up

Six people are dressed up in traditional costumes from around the world, but their lower halves are all mixed up! Use the stickers to put the right legs on the right person.

Mexico   Spain   Greece

Japan   Russia   Tahiti

Beach vacation word search

Can you find all these words in the puzzle?

sand

sunscreen

sunshade

bucket

seashore

towel

rocks

hat

book

shovel

```
a b h z p a s y k t n c
o n a o n t w s e l z i
s c t t g n e f e m e r
u k t s u n s c r e e n
n l r o c k s m l o r o
s t f o r b r u e r s s
h o s e a s h o r e a h
a w u a g j r l y c n o
d e m r t s b n e p d v
e l h l p b o e t e i e
t r b z s g o a e d e l
a e l b u c k e t h h b
```

Take a break

Q: Where do math teachers go on vacation?
A: Times Square!

Q: Why did the librarian get thrown off the airplane?
A: It was overbooked.

Q: Why did the robot go on vacation?
A: It needed to recharge its batteries.

Fast rafts

Which one of these rafts is the fastest? Do the math to find out.
The highest number is the quickest.

2 + 3 + 5
= ◯

5 + 8 - 4
= ◯

8 + 3 + 2
= ◯

Going on a picnic

Sam and Ellie are going on a picnic. Check the list against the picture
and circle anything in the list you think they've forgotten.

apple	picnic blanket
pear	bottle of lemonade
bread	potato chips
melon	plum cake
cheese	hard-boiled eggs
knife	glasses
plates	sandwiches

Vacation puppets

Make some simple puppets by following the instructions below.

You will need

- White cardstock or thick paper
- Pencil and tracing paper
- Coloring pencils or felt-tip pens
- Scissors
- Tape
- Craft sticks

1. Trace the pictures and transfer them onto the cardstock or paper, then color them in, or photocopy them.

2. Cut out the pictures.

3. Use tape to attach each picture to a craft stick.

4. Make up a story and act it out using your puppets!

Ice cream and popsicles

Unscramble the words to see which flavors are for sale, and write the answers in the boxes. Then follow the tangled lines to see which one the girl is going to buy.

hoocactle

wrestbrary

nailval

Winter vacation

Look at the picture and write T (true) or F (false) by the following statements:

◯ There are four children on sleds.

◯ Two people are wearing hats.

○ Three people are
on the ski lift.

○ There are four cable
cars in the picture.

Boating vacation differences

Can you spot five differences between these two pictures?

Shell spotting

On a beach vacation, you might find lots of pretty shells.
Fill in the missing letters in the words to discover which ones
this boy has found. The first one has been done for you.

murex

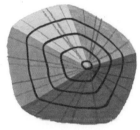

b_rn_cle

c_ckl_

mu__el

raz_r cl_m

c_nch

Vacation invitation

Choose from the picture stickers in the center of the book to illustrate this story.

One day, the mail carrier   brought a

postcard   from Mr Brown

asking his grandchildren,   Joe and Eva, to stay

at his house   during the spring vacation.

The children jumped for joy,   and

in the blink of an eye   their suitcases were packed!

"Taxi, are you free?" The taxi

took them to the station. The children bought train

tickets   and hopped on the train...

Odd pagoda out

If you go on vacation to Asia, you will see temples called pagodas. They have tiered roofs and are very beautiful. Which one of these is the odd one out?

Places to stay

Can you find all these places to stay when you are on vacation?

villa

cottage

tent

motel

chalet

hut

cabin

lodge

hotel

a p s t r e t a n m f
d v c k c i n g a c f
c i l l h o t e l o s
h l m o t e l j k t e
a l w d t a m b e t l
l a f g i b n u r a t
e m s e g i c k h g e
t g u a e y e a u e n
g g s l y n g m t u t
c a b i n a c e t p d

Winter wear

Draw lines to connect the squares with the person who's wearing the item shown.

Sailboat coloring

Color in this picture of a boy sailing his boat.

Word games

Look at the picture and complete these words using letters from the word **vacation**.

ha_
sk_s
glo_es
fl_g
c_ble _ar
d_wnhill
s_owy

Vacation fun

Q: Where do sheep go on vacation?
A: The baaaaahamas.

Q: Why was the family so tired after returning
from a summer vacation?
A: They flew all the way home.

Q: What did the beach say to the people who
came back for another vacation?
A: Long time no sea.

All around the world

Can you fill in the missing letters to label these continents? Choose from **a**, **e**, **i**, **o**, or **u**. Then find stickers in the center pages that match the picture outlines on the map.

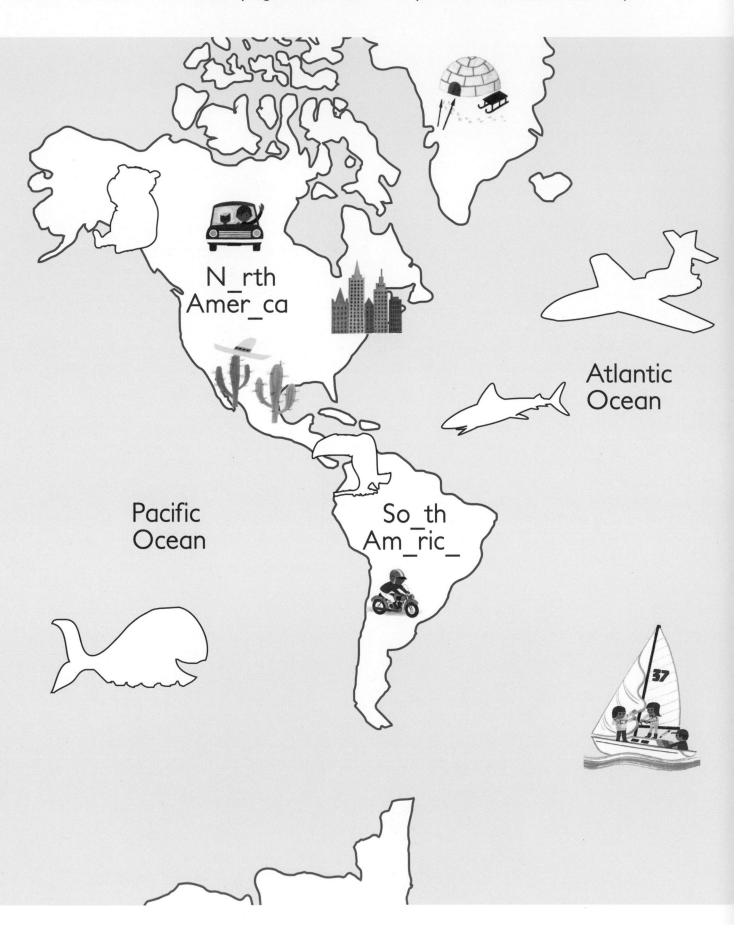

N_rth Amer_ca

Atlantic Ocean

Pacific Ocean

So_th Am_ric_

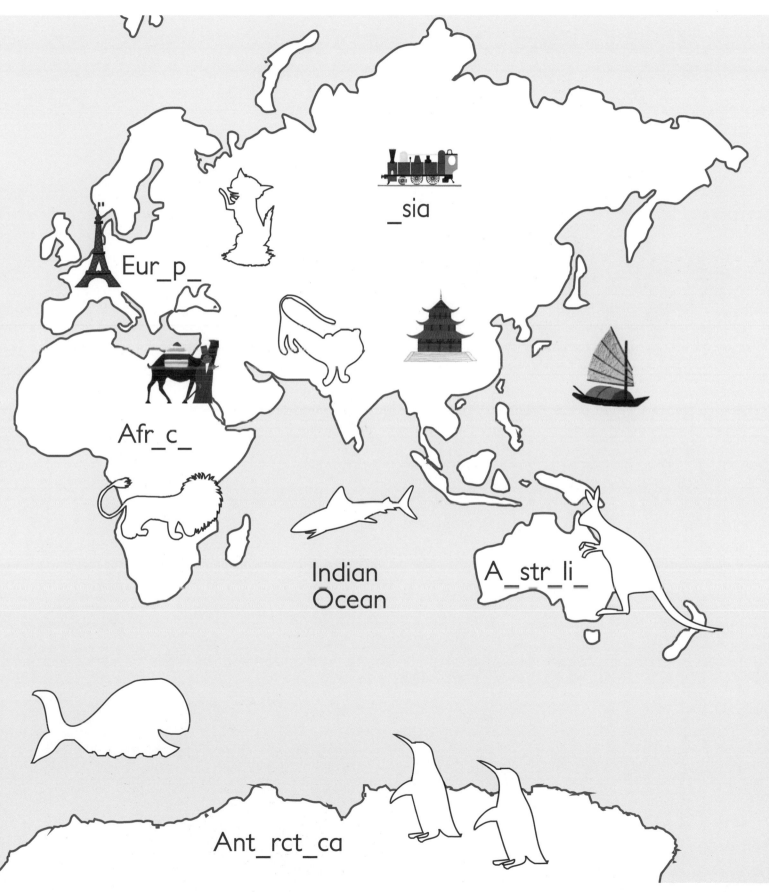

_sia

Eur_p_

Afr_c_

Indian
Ocean

A_str_li_

Ant_rct_ca

29

Missing pieces

This seashore scene is missing six details, shown in the circles below. Can you spot where each one should go? Write the numbers in the spaces or use the stickers.

1

2

3

4

5

6

Going scuba diving

Tom and Lola are going scuba diving on their vacation. Can you work out
what they might see under water by filling in the missing letters?

_r_b

l_bs_er

st_rf_sh

oct_pu_

s_el_s

f_s_

Dotty tree house

Join the dots to reveal this tree house and then color in the picture.

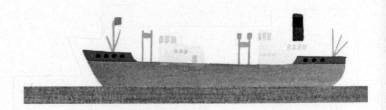

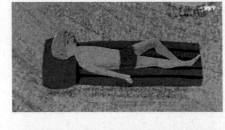

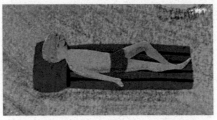

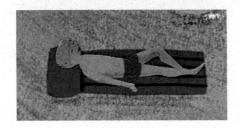

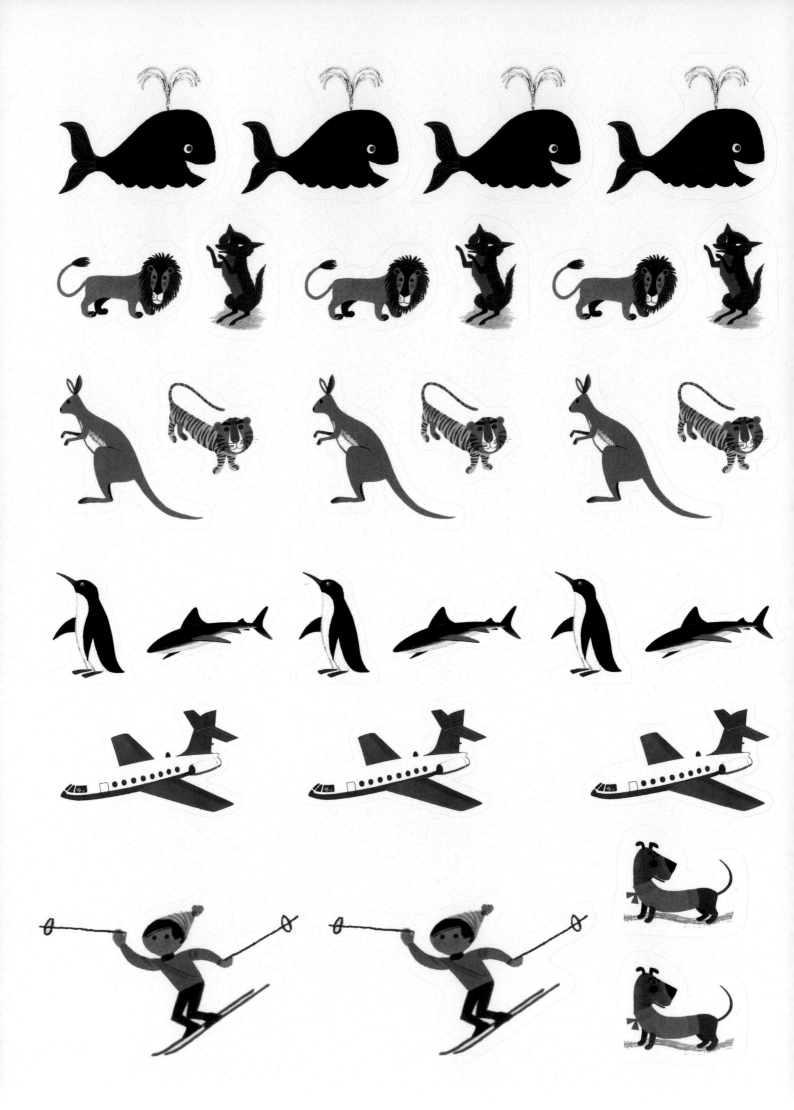

campsite   fun   sleeping bags   camping   campfire

tent   stick   ball   car   weekend

To the bridge

Help the gondolier get his passengers to the Rialto Bridge in Venice. Can you name any of the buildings he's going to pass on the way? Choose from the list and write the numbers in the circles. Number 5 has been done for you.

1 igloo   4 skyscrapers

2 pagoda   5 Rialto Bridge

3 Eiffel Tower

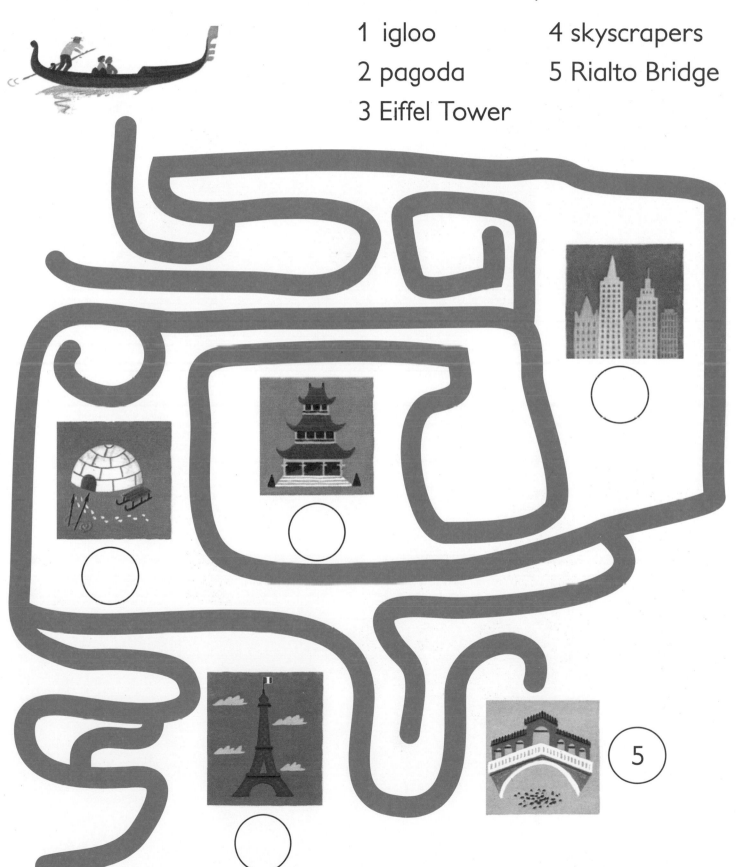

Spot the difference

Can you spot the five differences between these two pictures?

In the park

These people are having fun in the park. Count up how many toy boats, balloons, and children there are and write your answers in the circles.

◯ toy boats   ◯ balloons   ◯ children

Find the downhill ski route

Can you help the skier find a way around the poles to the finish? You need to weave in and out between each flag. Don't miss any out! The beginning of the route has been started off for you. Add some stickers from the center of the book if you like.

Start

Finish

Dotty boat

Join the dots to show a small sailboat on the water and then color it in.

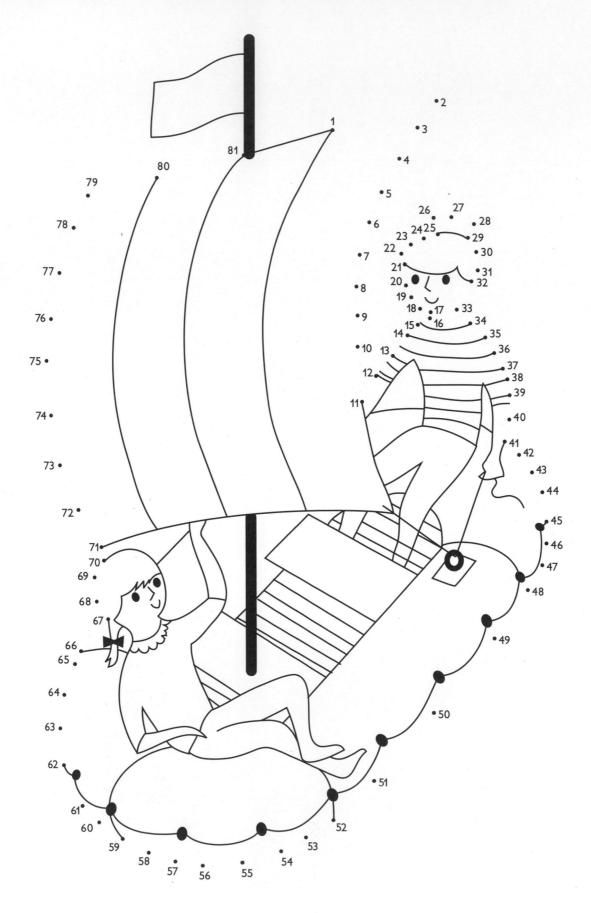

Downhill race

Which of these four skiers is going to win this race? Do the math to find out.
The one with the highest number wins.

7+2+3

= ◯

3+5-2

= ◯

9+1-3

= ◯

5+6+2

= ◯

Odd ones out

Two of these bobble hats are different from the others. Can you spot them?

Climbing vacation

Lots of people go on climbing vacations. Can you find the following equipment in this picture? Circle each one.

boots

helmet

ropes

goggles

gloves

Look in the box for the following and label them A, B, or C:

A pitons (tools that help your ropes hang on to the rock)

B ice pick

C ice hammer

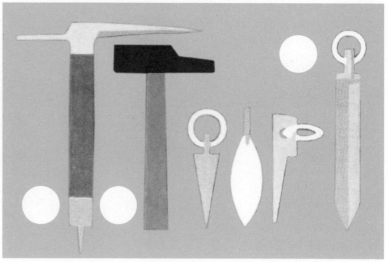

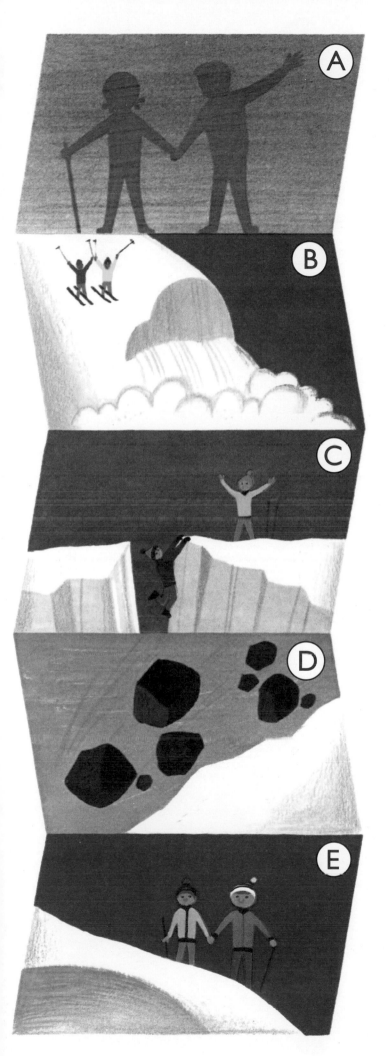

Vacation hazards

Sometimes things can go wrong when exploring the mountains! Which of the following best describes each of these pictures? Write in A to E. The first one has been done for you.

(A) We're lost in the mist!

( ) Look out, falling rocks!

( ) Which way now?

( ) Help me up out of here!

( ) Oh no, avalanche!

Three in a row

Find stickers of cars, trains, bicycles, and boats in the center pages and use them to fill the gaps. Try to make three in a row, either down or across.

Vacation humour

Q: Where do bees go on vacation?
A: Stingapore.

Q: What travels around the world
but stays in one corner?
A: A stamp.

Q: What do spooky creatures send
their friends when on vacation?
A: Ghostcards.

Q: Why didn't the elephant pack a suitcase
for his winter break?
A: Because he used a trunk.

Indoor activities word search

What can you do on vacation when the weather's not great? See if you can find the following activities to do and places to go to.

games	crafts
play cards	music
puzzles	cooking
drawing	museum
reading	movies

```
c d r a w i n g k i w s
g t a e p u r q e h q g
a f i t l l m s r l o j
m r p w a l o h i c m c
e f u e y b v l o m t o
s i z e c l i c d u x o
e m z d a q e r s s p k
v u l r r g s a m e z i
d s e l d b e f e u s n
c i s e s f s t n m f g
g c l h v m b s v s y k
k r e a d i n g k j n t
```

Island race

Which of these vacationers is going to reach the island first?
Follow the tangled lines to find out.

Summer camping trip

Choose words from the sticker pages in the center of the book to complete this story.

One fine summer's day, Jack's parents said, "Let's go [_____]!" "I don't want

to," replied Jack. "Camping's cold and horrid! It's no fun." "Don't worry, Jack," said his

dad. "Your mum and I are great campers. We'll look after you and we'll all have lots

of [_____]!" So they packed up the [_____] and things to keep

them dry and warm. They took plenty of food and water, packed everything in the

[_____] and drove off. Around midday, they arrived at a lovely [_____]

in the middle of a wood. Jack helped his parents put up the tent. That was fun! He went

to the play area and made a new friend called Jake. They rode their bicycles, kicked a

[_____], and ate snacks together. That was fun too! Later, Jack's father made

a [_____]. Jack stuck a marshmallow on the end of a [_____] and

poked it in the fire to melt. The family cooked their dinner, and Jack helped with the

washing up. That wasn't so much fun but it had to be done! Then they all got into their

[_____] and fell asleep in the tent. The next day, when Jack woke up, it was time

to pack up and leave. But Jack didn't want to go. "Why do we have to go home?" he said.

"Camping's so much fun! Can we come again next [_____]?"

Happy campers

Camping is a lot of fun, but you need to take care. Put a check in the circles when you think it's a good idea and put an 'x' in the circles if you think it's something you shouldn't do. Can you think of anything else? Write on the lines below.

○ play music late at night

○ bring warm clothes and raincoats

○ leave food out

○ pitch your tent on level ground

○ put your tent up in the dark

○ leave a campfire unattended

○ practice putting your tent up before you go

○ go for a walk in the woods on your own

○ take your trash away with you

_____   _____

_____   _____

_____   _____

Winter vacation fun

Look at the picture of this snowy scene. How many people are skiing?
How many people are skating? Write your answers in the circles below.

 skiers  skaters

Boy racers

Do the math to see which sled is going the fastest.
Write your answers in the circles provided.

4 + 2 + 3
= ◯

6 + 4 - 2
= ◯

9 - 3 + 5
= ◯

Winter sports word search

Can you find these winter
sports in the puzzle?

skating

skiing

sledding

snowboarding

ice hockey

ice climbing

curling

e	t	s	l	e	d	d	i	n	g	r	e
a	t	i	e	u	v	c	q	h	e	w	s
b	a	c	a	n	l	n	s	r	x	o	k
k	r	e	w	n	i	t	z	b	q	u	a
q	y	h	r	b	l	t	b	y	t	l	t
s	n	o	w	b	o	a	r	d	i	n	g
k	s	c	d	a	l	b	y	l	b	p	x
i	h	k	s	k	a	t	i	n	g	u	w
i	i	e	l	o	t	a	q	e	r	s	i
n	s	y	e	l	l	s	m	n	g	h	s
g	d	g	h	d	c	u	r	l	i	n	g
r	i	c	e	c	l	i	m	b	i	n	g

Make a pathway

These children are on their way to a vacation cottage. Help them get there by choosing the shapes A, B, or C to complete the bends in the path and drawing them in the boxes. One has been done for you.

The very heavy suitcase

Romeo the dog is going on vacation. Can you match the captions to the pictures?
Choose from the options on the right. The first one has been done for you.

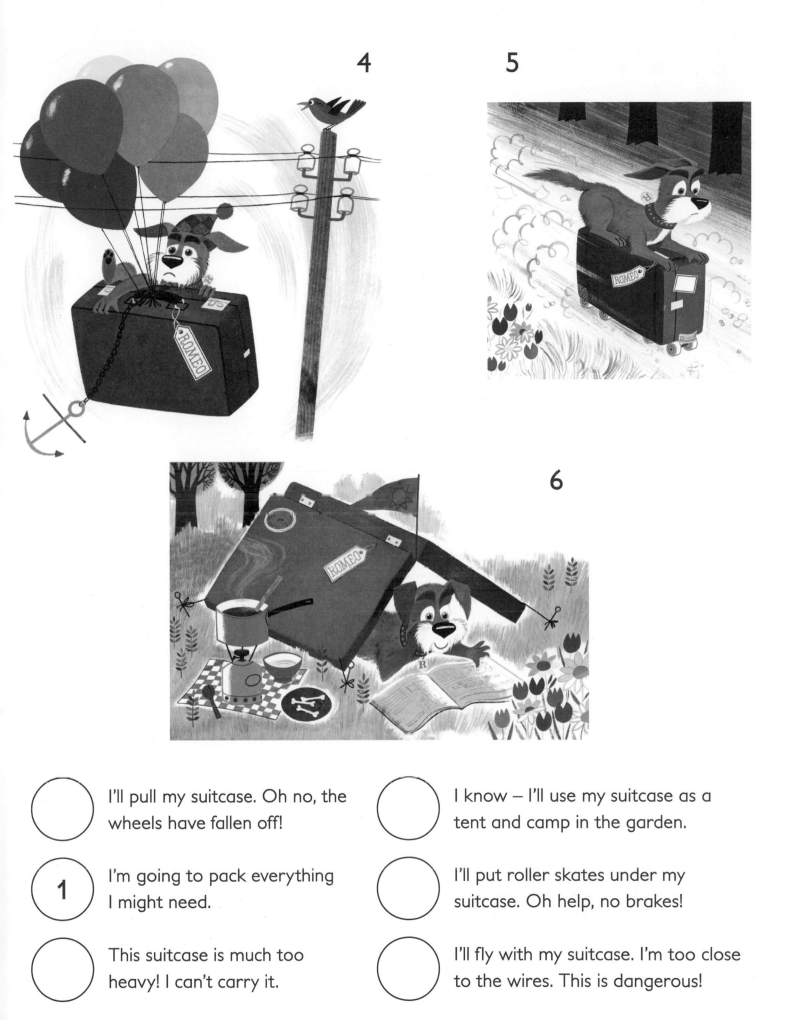

4

5

6

◯ I'll pull my suitcase. Oh no, the wheels have fallen off!

◯ I know – I'll use my suitcase as a tent and camp in the garden.

1 I'm going to pack everything I might need.

◯ I'll put roller skates under my suitcase. Oh help, no brakes!

◯ This suitcase is much too heavy! I can't carry it.

◯ I'll fly with my suitcase. I'm too close to the wires. This is dangerous!

Disappearing train

This train is disappearing! Draw the other half of this train car back in, then color it. Add some passengers to the train car too.

Spot the difference

Can you spot five differences between these two pictures?

Back home from vacation

Look at the picture and write **T** (true) or **F** (false) by the following statements:

There are 11 people in the picture. ◯   There are two dogs. ◯

There are three bags on the roof of the car. ◯

Match the bags to the luggage carts and add up the numbers in the circles to see who is pushing the heaviest load. Draw a circle round that person.

② ④ ③ ⑦ ⑤ ② ⑥

Vacation essentials (pages 2–3)

coloring pencils and notebook

On a summer vacation
sun hat
bathing suit
sunscreen

On a winter vacation
gloves
warm hat
scarf

clothes

shoes and socks

umbrella

ball

hairbrush

suitcase

camera

toothbrush

toothpaste

Beach fun (pages 4–5)
people = 18
boats = 4
balls = 3

Getting around (page 6)
taxi, bicycle, walking, boat, car, scooter

Going on vacation by train (page 7)
people on the train = 12
people on the platform = 7
dogs = 4

Name the place (pages 8–9)

Beach game (page 11)

Odd numbers = red   Even numbers = blue

Beach vacation word search (page 13)

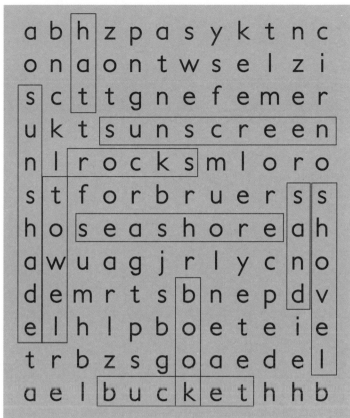

Costume mix-up (page 12)

Fast rafts (page 14)

2 + 3 + 5 = 10

5 + 8 - 4 = 9

8 + 3 + 2 = 13 (quickest)

Going on a picnic (page 15)

They have forgotten to pack the potato chips and hard-boiled eggs.

Ice cream and popsicles (page 17)

The flavors are:
chocolate
strawberry
vanilla

Winter vacation (pages 18–19)

T (true): there are 4 children on sleds.
F (false): 9 people are wearing hats.
T (true): 3 people are on the ski lift.
T (true): there are 4 cable cars.

Boating vacation differences (page 20)

Shell spotting (page 21)

murex, barnacle, cockle,
mussel, razor clam, conch

Vacation invitation (page 22)

One day, the mail carrier brought a postcard from Mr Brown asking his grandchildren, Joe and Eva, to stay at his house during the spring vacation. The children jumped for joy, and in the blink of an eye their suitcases were packed! 'Taxi, are you free?' The taxi took them to the station. The children bought train tickets and hopped on the train...

Odd pagoda out (page 23)

Places to stay (page 23)

a	p	s	t	r	e	t	a	n	m	f
d	v	c	k	c	i	n	g	a	c	f
c	i	l	l	h	o	t	e	l	o	s
h	l	m	o	t	e	l	j	k	t	e
a	l	w	d	t	a	m	b	e	t	l
l	a	f	g	i	b	n	u	r	a	t
e	m	s	e	g	i	c	k	h	g	e
t	g	u	a	e	y	e	a	u	e	n
g	g	s	l	y	n	g	m	t	u	t
c	a	b	i	n	a	c	e	t	p	d

Missing pieces (page 30)

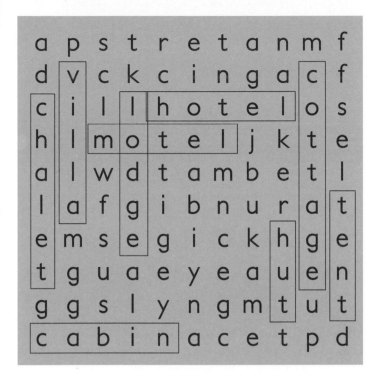

Winter wear (pages 24–25)

Going scuba diving (page 31)

crab, lobster, starfish
octopus, shells, fish

Word games (page 27)

hat, skis, gloves, flag, cable car,
downhill, snowy

To the bridge (page 33)

All around the world (pages 28–29)

North America, South America, Europe,
Africa, Asia, Australia, Antarctica

Spot the difference
(page 34)

Downhill race (page 39)

7 + 2 + 3 = 12

3 + 5 - 2 = 6

9 + 1 - 3 = 7

5 + 6 + 2 = 13 (winner)

In the park (page 35)

toy boats = 4

balloons = 9

children = 7

Odd ones out (page 39)

Find the downhill ski route
(pages 36–37)

Mountain vacation
(page 40)

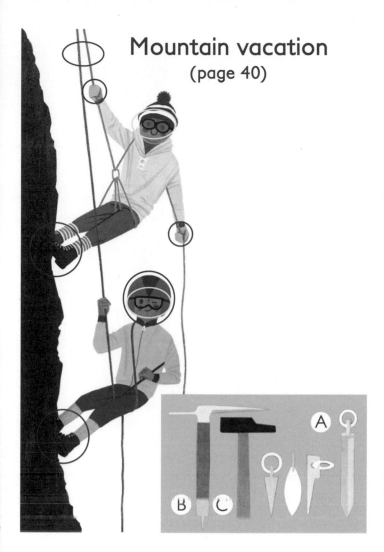

Three in a row
(pages 42–43)

Vacation hazards
(page 41)

(A) We're lost in the mist!

(D) Look out, falling rocks!

(E) Which way now?

(C) Help me up out of here!

(B) Oh no, avalanche!

Indoor activities (page 44)

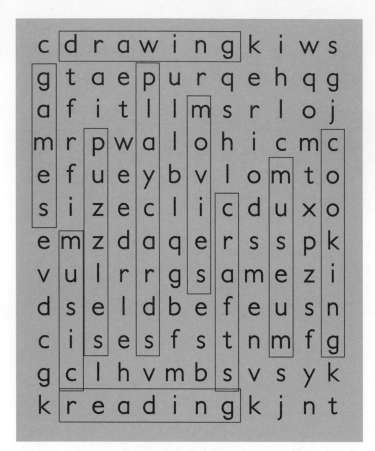

Island race (page 45)

Summer camping trip (page 46)

One fine summer's day, Jack's parents said, "Let's go [camping]!" "I don't want to," replied Jack. "Camping's cold and horrid! It's no fun." "Don't worry, Jack," said his dad. "Your mum and I are great campers. We'll look after you and we'll all have lots of [fun]!" So they packed up the [tent] and things to keep them dry and warm. They took plenty of food and water, packed everything in the [car] and drove off. Around midday, they arrived at a lovely [campsite] in the middle of a wood. Jack helped his parents put up the tent. That was fun! He went to the play area and made a new friend called Jake. They rode their bicycles, kicked a [ball], and ate snacks together. That was fun too! Later, Jack's father made a [campfire]. Jack stuck a marshmallow on the end of a [stick] and poked it in the fire to melt. The family cooked their dinner, and Jack helped with the washing up. That wasn't so much fun but it had to be done! Then they all got into their [sleeping bags] and fell asleep in the tent. The next day, when Jack woke up, it was time to pack up and leave. But Jack didn't want to go. "Why do we have to go home?" he said. "Camping's so much fun! Can we come again next [weekend]?"

Happy campers
(page 47)

- ✗ play music late at night
- ✓ bring warm clothes and raincoats
- ✗ leave food out
- ✗ pitch your tent on level ground
- ✗ put your tent up in the dark
- ✗ leave a campfire unattended
- ✓ practice putting your tent up before you go
- ✗ go for a walk in the woods on your own
- ✓ take your trash away with you

Winter vacation fun
(page 48)

There are 4 skiers.
There are 3 skaters.

Boy racers (page 49)

$4 + 2 + 3 = 9$

$6 + 4 - 2 = 8$

$9 - 3 + 5 = 11$ (fastest)

Winter sports word search
(page 49)

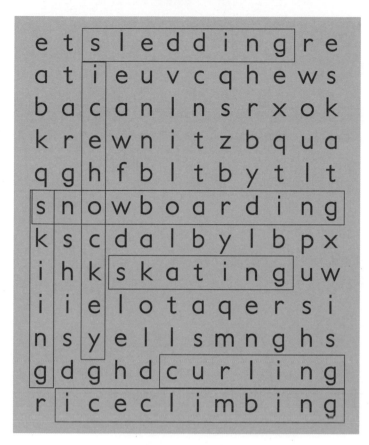

Spot the difference
(page 54)

Make a pathway
(pages 50–51)

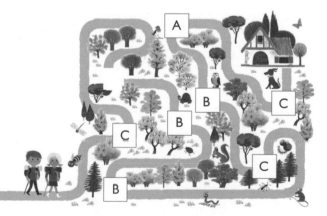

Back home from vacation
(page 55)

F (false): there are 17 people in the picture.

F (false): there is 1 dog in the picture.

T (true): there are 3 bags on the car roof.

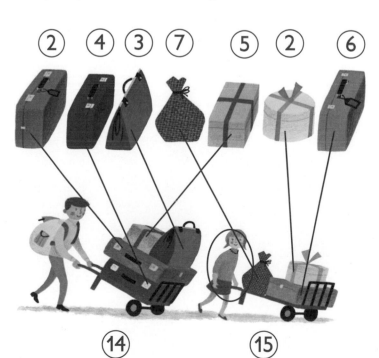

The very heavy suitcase
(pages 52–53)

3 — I'll pull my suitcase. Oh no, the wheels have fallen off!

1 — I'm going to pack everything I might need.

2 — This suitcase is much too heavy! I can't carry it.

6 — I know – I'll use my suitcase as a tent and camp in the garden.

5 — I'll put roller skates under my suitcase. Oh help, no brakes!

4 — I'll fly with my suitcase. I'm too close to the wires. This is dangerous!

First published 2020 by Button Books, an imprint of Guild of Master Craftsman Publications Ltd, Castle Place, 166 High Street, Lewes, East Sussex, BN7 1XU, UK. Text © GMC Publications Ltd, 2020. Copyright in the Work © GMC Publications Ltd, 2020. Illustrations © 2020 A.G. & RicoBel. ISBN 978 1 78708 055 3. Distributed by Publishers Group West in the United States. All rights reserved. The right of Alain Grée to be identified as the illustrator of this work has been asserted in accordance with the Copyright, Designs, and Patents Act 1988, sections 77 and 78. No part of this publication may be reproduced, stored in a retrieval system, or transmitted in any form or by any means without the prior permission of the publisher and copyright owner. While every effort has been made to obtain permission from the copyright holders for all material used in this book, the publishers will be pleased to hear from anyone who has not been appropriately acknowledged and to make the correction in future reprints. The publishers and author can accept no legal responsibility for any consequences arising from the application of information, advice, or instructions given in this publication. A catalog record for this book is available from the British Library. Publisher: Jonathan Bailey. Production: Jim Bulley, Jo Pallett. Senior Project Editor: Sara Harper. Managing Art Editor: Gilda Pacitti. Designer: Ginny Zeal. Color origination by GMC Reprographics. Printed and bound in China. Warning! Choking hazard—small parts. Not suitable for children under 3 years.